Managing Difficult Relationships

Achieving Workable Compromise through Negotiation

Copyright (c) George P Boulden

All Rights Reserved

No part of this book may be reproduced in any form, by photocopying or by any electronic or mechanical means, Including information storage or retrieval systems, without permission in writing from both the copyright owner and the publisher of this book.

ISBN: 9781709255816

First Published January 2009

ALA INTERNATIONAL PUBLISHING

Lutterworth, England – alapub@ala-international.com

Email – george.boulden@ala-international.com

Web site – www.ala-international.com

Ed 8 June 2020

Contents

Managing Difficult Relationships - 1
Contents - 2
Synopsis - 3
Acknowledgements - 4
Creating Win / Win Relationships - 6
Managing Relationships - 9
Be aware of what is going on - 10
Understand the problem - 17
Know your desired Outcome - 19
Move to your Adult ego state - 21
Interrupt their Pattern - 25
Use the 3 step Assertiveness Technique - 28
Developing your Relationship Management Skills - 31
Benchmarking - 34
Analysing your assessment to identify development needs - 37
Barriers to Effective Interpersonal Relationships - 45
Create a development plan - 48
Implementing your Plan - 51
Implementing your Plan - 56
Continuous assessment - 58
Annex A - Profiles of Difficult People - 60
Further Reading - 70

Synopsis

All of us experience difficulties with our relationships from time to time. There are two main reasons for this, sometimes its 'style' the way I want to do something is different from the way you want to do it and sometimes its 'substance', you and I want something different. This book;

1. Explains the basis of win / win relationships
2. Offers an 'structured' approach to managing relationships
3. Uses self-assessment to enable the reader to identify their development needs
4. Identifies a number of different types of 'difficult behaviour' and provides guidance on how to work with them.

Being able to manage difficult relationships is a key skill for everyone with the ambition to succeed.

Acknowledgements

I would like to begin by acknowledging the great debt of gratitude I owe to Professor Reginald (Reg) Revans, the founder of the Action Learning movement. We met in 1974 when he was planning his first Action Learning programme in GEC. At the time of our first meeting I had recently transferred from line management into a management development role. I was very aware that mature managers did not respond well to 'teaching' and was searching for ways of creating learning opportunities. Over lunch Reg shared his ideas with me and I was sold; thirty-five years later I am still a convinced action learner. He introduced me to Alan Lawlor who pioneered Own Job Action Learning in the West Midlands and the three of us created Action Learning Associates (ALA) Intentional in 1980 to promote the application of Action Learning. My relationship with Reg continued until his death in 2003.

I would also like to acknowledge my good friends Malcolm Farnsworth, John Cooper and Professor Steve Iman of Cal Poly Pomona CA.

Malcolm, who as Principal of the Marconi Staff Development Centre in Chelmsford, gave me the chance of a new career in management development which I have pursued for a very stimulating thirty-five years.

John, who I worked with at Dunchurch Staff College, is a natural 'action learner' as anyone who has used or experienced the marvellous business simulations he created will testify and generous to a fault with everything he did. For me John is one of the unsung heroes of Action Learning and deserves to be recognised as such.

Steve for his encouragement and enormous contribution to the publication of the book; without Steve's guiding hand it would probably never have seen the light of day'

Finally I would like to thank the many hundreds of participants and clients from around the globe who I have learned with and from over the years. It has been a great privilege to know you, thank you all.

George P Boulden - May 2015

Creating Win / Win Relationships

It may help, but you don't have to like me, to work with me

Meaningful relationships are based on rapport. Rapport is the ability of one human being to create harmony between themselves and others either individually or in groups. To establish rapport we must align our values selves with the values of those who we wish to influence. This means identifying something that we have in common and using this to create 'rapport'. Thus the 'stranger' moves from being a stranger to being 'one of us' and we can move on to understand and satisfy other needs.

Rapport is a 'natural' process between people who are like us. People who have similar backgrounds for example find it easy to create mutually satisfying relationships because they have 'things in common' and thus the basis for rapport. It is however more difficult to develop such relationships with people from different backgrounds, because we 'assume' they are different and they probably are.

Some people have a natural ability to develop rapport with almost everyone. This means that they are able to work effectively with many different types of people. The 'natural' sales person for example has this ability. How do they do it? By looking not at differences but for things they do have in common; a love of cars, good food, travel, sport, a job etc. Once these shared values are established it is possible to extend the relationship.

> *Some years ago I was a member of a Bridge group. We met one evening a week during the winter in each other's homes and played Bridge. We stopped playing around Easter and began again in the autumn with little contact in between; the thing we had in common was the Bridge and an evening's companionship. However, because we had rapport through the Bridge group, if we needed something from each other, we had a positive relationship that we could and did use from time to time to get help with other things.*

Relationships without rapport are difficult because they lack trust. If we focus on the differences between us we will never create win / win situations. The 'natural' sales person has no barriers to creating relationships. For them, everyone is a (potential) customer. Finding common ground is the key to their success. However, whilst most of us are not sales people in the accepted sense, we are all 'sellers' in our own way, because we all have to 'sell' ourselves. For us, everyone we interact with has a part to play in our success. We need to be able, like the 'natural' sales person, to develop win / win relationships with those we interface with, not just those who we like.

This book provides guidance on how to create and maintain the relationships necessary for all of us to optimise our personal performance. It does this by providing a step-by-step process for managing difficult relationships effectively by breaking the other party's normal pattern of behaviour and engaging in open and honest communication.

Managing Relationships

The approach set out in this book is based a successful development programme we designed for a client. The company had identified that there were significant performance problems in the organisation due, they believed, to poor 'relationship management'. They wanted something that would encourage their managers to recognise the value of 'win / win relationships.

1. An understanding of the steps that 'expert' relationship managers use to create win / win outcomes.
2. The skills that they use to manage their relationships and
3. The way they assess themselves at the end of an interaction in order to continually improve their performance

The following seven step process provides a logical structure for managing our relationships. It allows us to lift our interpersonal behaviours from the subconscious into the conscious and thus creates the conditions for us to respond rather than react to the behaviour of others.

1. Be aware of what is going on
2. Understand the problem
3. Know your Outcome
4. Move to your Adult ego state
5. Interrupt their pattern
6. Use the 3 step Assertiveness Technique
7. Maintain the relationship

Be aware of what is going on

It may sound obvious but the first thing to do when you encounter a difficult interpersonal situation is to identify in what way specifically the person you are dealing with is difficult to relate to. This involves:

Listening to the 'meta message'

Messages are transmitted at two levels in face-to-face communication. The surface message, which is conveyed in the actual words that people use and the underlying meaning (the meta message) which is transmitted in the tone of voice, body posture, breathing pattern and facial expressions the communicator uses. Of these two levels the meta message is the most important in conveying meaning: it's not what you say it's the way that you say it that matters most. In fact the research suggests that over 80% of the meaning of the messages people communicate is contained in the meta level.

The meaning of a simple sentence can be changed simply by altering voice tone, posture, breathing pattern, and facial expression. The meta message tells us whether or not a person is: confident or uncertain, clear or confused, agreeing or disagreeing, angry or happy, determined or lacking drive and much more besides.

So, for example, when someone says; "Where's that report?" If it is said in:

1. A critical tone of voice, arms folded, and staring eyes the message is Critical Parent.
2. An even tone, upright and relaxed posture, and calm gaze the message Adult
3. A fretful tone, down cast eyes, quick breaths the message is from a worried Child?

Paying attention to the meta level of the communication and noticing exactly what the person is doing when they are being 'difficult' is a vital first step in the process of learning how to cope with them more effectively. If the underlying message isn't properly understood it is very easy to jump to an incorrect conclusion and therefore to make an inappropriate response. For example, sometimes when people say they want help the voice tone makes it clear that what they are really asking for is sympathy, rather than solutions. Giving advice when what is really wanted is comfort will not create the rapport necessary for a successful dialogue.

Note. We are all experts at interpreting each other's meta level language. The problem is that for most of us this is a 'subconscious competency'. We therefore tend to react to what we perceive rather than responding to it. Improving the way we communicate starts with changing subconscious recognition into conscious recognition and subconscious reaction into an appropriate response.

Listen to the specific words that people use

The actual words that people use may only account for as little as 20% of the meaning that is conveyed in face to face communication but words are of course still important so it pays to make sure that we have understood them properly. This involves:

Make things 'concrete'. When talking people use:

1. Fat, abstract words (which have a number of possible meanings) e.g. Good, Nice, Crime, Big
2. Thin, concrete words (which you can visualise and touch and have precise meanings) e.g. Steam, Robbery, 5%

Big words can hide misunderstandings, effective communicators, therefore, turn vague, fuzzy abstract words into specific words by asking 'what specifically' the person has in mind when they use a generalisation. E.g.

"What, specifically, do you mean by a 'large' pay rise?

It is usually a good idea to 'soften' this type of 'challenge' to be specific because many times the person will not have thought through what they do really mean and they can be startled by being asked to explain themselves in detail. 'Soft front ends' take the form of:-

"I was just wondering what, specifically, do you mean by a 'large' pay rise?

"Tell me, I'm curious to know what, specifically, do you mean by a 'large' pay rise?

Naturally, this needs to be delivered with an 'Adult' voice tone and posture to be effective.

Identifying sensory based language

There are three main ways in which people prefer to think. These 'thinking styles' relate to the main senses, and each thinking style is reflected in the words that people choose when speaking; this is what we mean by sensory based language.

Some people are primarily visually oriented and when they talk they tend to use words like: "I see what you mean," "I get the picture," "I'm not clear what you're getting at." Others have an auditory or hearing orientation and favour phrases such as: "I hear what you say," "That sounds good," "You're not in tune with the rest of the group." The third category is centred on the sense of feeling and touch: "That doesn't feel right," "Can we get a handle on that?" "Let's get to grips with this problem." Looking out for, listening for or picking up on these speech patterns and then using similar types of phrases, makes rapport easier to establish and the message easier to understand.

When people use sensory-based language they tend to move their eyes in set patterns. By noticing these eye movements we can 'tune in' more easily to the persons language patterns. For example when a person moves their eyes upward and left or upward and right they are usually thinking in 'pictures'. Some of these movements are very fast so if we are not alert we can miss them. It is also important to realise that the most common pattern of what is called 'eye accessing clues' as shown below is accurate for 80% of the population i.e. one in five people adopt different patterns when thinking in pictures, sounds, or feelings. The 'normal' pattern of eye accessing clues is based on their left and their right.

Eye Movement	Thinking Process
Up-Right	Inventing, constructing a picture
Up-Left	Remembering a picture
Level- Right	Inventing, constructing a sound
Level- Left	Remembering a sound
Down-Right	Experiencing a feeling or sensation
Down-Left	Conversation with oneself – Self-talk

Listening to the words people use is important because sometimes people find each other 'difficult' for no other reason than they literally don't understand the point that the other person is trying to make. For example if someone:

1. is talking about 'doing something quickly' this may mean in five minutes to one person and in two weeks to another.

2. uses a lot of visual based language (show, reveal, expose, clarify) they may find it hard to see what point a person who uses a lot of feeling based words (touch, shock, impact, move) is trying to impress upon them.

Checking you have got it right

Imagine a situation in which you are having a conversation with someone. You are listening at the 'meta level'. As you do this you detect a particular tone in their voice and you interpret this to mean that they are angry with you. The question then becomes "have you got it right?" does that tone of voice really mean that they are cross with you or does it mean something quite different e.g. they are late for another meeting and just want to finish their business with you quickly, in which case the tone might mean 'urgency' rather than 'anger'.

Most people can, with practice, become very skilled at consciously interpreting the correct meaning of the 'meta level message' but even with someone they know well most 'experts' still test their assumptions from time to time just to make sure that they are on the right track. This checking or testing can be done by:-

Questioning

> I KEPT SIX HONEST SERVING MEN
> THEY TAUGHT ME ALL I KNEW
> THEIR NAMES ARE **What**, AND **Why** AND **When**;
> AND **How** AND **Where** AND **Who**...
> RUDYARD KIPLING

As Kipling said in his famous poem questions are the best 'tool' for ensuring that both parties have fully understood what the other is trying to say and to make sure that the 'full story' has been uncovered. Some useful questions are:-

Feelings Commentary Questions to check the person's emotional state e.g. by asking something like "How do you feel about that?" or "I get the feeling that you're annoyed, is that true?"

Reflected Questions to gain extra information by 'playing back' as a question, a statement made by the other party. If the employee says, for instance: "I've got some disciplinary problems in my section". The manager might reply: "You see discipline as a real problem, then?" or even more simply, the manager may just echo the key words: "Discipline problems?"

Summarising

At the end of a discussion and/or at any significant point in the conversation, summarise the main points. This provides an opportunity to test the understanding of both parties and agree what has been said. Summarising should be done by the person who is receiving the information. This enables the giver to assess how well they have understood the points being made.

Understand the problem

Once you are aware of what specifically is happening in the difficult relationship the next step is to define what the real problem is. It could be that the person in question isn't really 'difficult' at all. It could be that there is a mismatch in communication style which can be cleared up by specifying what each person really means by (i) using concrete terms (ii) matching their sensory based language.

If you are working with a truly 'difficult' person the Transactional Analysis model suggests that they are that way because they work from the Parent or Child ego state when an Adult approach would be more appropriate. This is because, in childhood the person has learned to use a Parent or Child pattern in response to difficult situations and now as grown-ups they continue to use these patterns even though they damage their relationships with others quite unnecessarily. Identifying the 'real' problem as a Parent or Child pattern helps us to understand better the sorts of things we need to do to move the situation forward. Consider for example, the person who when faced with a situation that they feel uncomfortable in goes into their:

Critical Parent ego state bullies and barracks the other person in the hope that they will be pushed into their Child ego state and give way. The person who 'attacks' in this way is trying to make their 'victim' feel like a small child who has annoyed their teacher. The response here is to show the aggressor that you can't be 'squashed' and to insist on negotiating a solution.

Adaptive Child ego state, using its rebellious aspect explodes in a blind rage, like the toddler whose parents won't do what he or she wants. The goal is to so startle the other person that they go into the compliant part of their Child ego state and psychologically (and maybe physically) run away. The approach is the same as that for a toddler who loses his temper: break off contact for a short while so they can regain some self-control and then start to reason with them and thereby bring them into the Adult.

Adaptive Child ego state, withdraws and become silent and unresponsive, refusing to give eye contact or do more than grunt one or two words when asked questions. Here the person is trying to get a Nurturing Parent response from the other party in the hope that they will feel unable to push and probe for proper answers. In this case the response is to avoid the temptation to be caring and polite and to ask a question and then wait in silence until it is answered. If no answer is forthcoming the next step is to tell them exactly what will happen to them if they keep their behaviour up, in much the same way as one might gently but firmly address a sullen, sulky child.

When identifying the real problem it's important to remember that although the difficult behaviours have childhood origins they are not being used by children. They are being used by grown-ups with all the experience and guile of a lifetime at their disposal. This means that some difficult people are very good indeed at their 'chosen' behaviour pattern; after all they have been practising it for many years. So part of the problem is usually the ability of the person seeking to change the relationship to summon up the energy, resourcefulness and flexibility needed to deal with the situation effectively, which brings us to the next step in the coping process.

See the section on, Further Reading for more information about Transactional Analysis.

Know your desired Outcome

The next step is to work out what your goal is in dealing with the difficult person. If you are taken completely by surprise then you may have to trust your instincts to settle upon an appropriate goal then and there. As long as you can stay in the Adult then your instinct will probably be more or less right. On most occasions, however, we have at least some chance to think about the sorts of results we want to get and when this is the case going through the following procedure can greatly help to clarify our thinking:

Step	Description
Aim for a specific result	What specifically do you want to happen? Where specifically do you want it? When specifically do you want it? With whom specifically do you want it?
Be positive	State your outcome in terms of what you do want rather than what you want to avoid. E.g. say "I want to be an ex smoker" not "I want to give up smoking"
See, hear & feel what you want	Mentally go into the future and (i) see what you will see (ii) hear what you will hear (iii) feel what you will feel when you have successfully achieved your outcome. This is a good test of whether you really do want the outcome and it also helps to make it very compelling. Notice what skills and abilities you will need to achieve the outcome e.g. a strong sense of determination. Find a time when you used these skills well e.g. recall an occasion when you were very determined and know that you already have the strengths you need to achieve your outcome.
Dove tail with other outcomes	How well does this outcome fit in with your other goals in your work and social life? Does this goal or maybe some of your other goals need to be 'reshaped' so they link together better? How well does your outcome fit with the needs and wants of the people who are important to you? Do you need to make adjustments to take their desires into account?
Entertain the long & short term issues	How well does the outcome support where you want to be in ten or twenty years' time? Does it fit with the direction you want your life to go in? What actions do you need to take in the short term to

	start to turn your outcome into reality? Are you prepared to do what is necessary to take these actions successfully? Write down what these actions are and when you will do them.

Move to your Adult ego state

One of the most important steps in the process for coping with difficult people is to gain and keep the mental state of being calm, rational, relaxed and resourceful. This means adopting the Adult ego state. This can be hard because the aim of the difficult person's behaviour is to push us out of this logical, objective frame of mind and into an emotional Parent or Child response. They seek to force us into feeling helpless, or caring, or judgemental etc. because then they, rather than us, set the tone and direction of the conversation.

So when provoked by a difficult person how can we keep our sense of perspective and stay 'in charge' of our feelings?

Forewarned is forearmed

Simply knowing that a difficult person is trying to manipulate you into an emotional response means that it is less likely to work than would otherwise be the case. Just by deciding to stay objective our ability to stay 'in the Adult' is increased.

Control your body posture

Think about what someone looks like when they are feeling 'down in the dumps'. Typically they gaze downwards, their mouth turns down at the corners, their breathing is shallow, their shoulders are hunched and their posture is slumped. Now think of someone who is on 'top of the world'. You probably see someone who is looking ahead, smiling, breathing high in the chest with the shoulders held slightly back and posture upright. If someone copies this 'on top of the world' posture and breathing pattern do you think they could feel depressed even if they wanted to? The answer for most people is no. If someone changes the way they stand and breathe they change the way they feel. This is one reason why people often find that walking helps them to sort things out. So one way of keeping in the Adult, even under trying circumstances, is to maintain an Adult posture and breathing pattern i.e. gaze ahead, body held relaxed and upright, breathing smooth, regular and even.

Control your mental focus

In this example what do you suppose the person who is down in the dumps is thinking about that is causing him / her to feel depressed? Maybe they are reflecting upon all the bad things that are going to happen and all the things that have gone 'wrong' or that could go wrong? What about the 'upbeat' person, what are they thinking about to cause them to feel good? Perhaps they are reflecting on the good things in a situation, or the possible options that they have before them and how things will turn out for the best? All of us have this choice of controlling our mental focus. We can choose to look for the positive things or the negative things in any situation. We can focus on failure or we can focus on the actions we can take to change things. We can also choose to focus on staying rational and objective in any situation and in doing so we can stay 'in the Adult' even when other people use their difficult behaviours on us.

Rehearse staying in the Adult

It is possible to mentally rehearse staying in the Adult by using the following procedure:

1. Identify when specifically a given person starts their 'difficult' behaviour and note down anything you see just before they start being difficult. E.g. maybe a manager has a particular look that comes on his face just before he starts shouting at people. Mentally store this image as a picture in your mind's eye.
2. In your mind's eye picture yourself with the difficult person and see and feel yourself being calm, relaxed and objective (i.e. staying in the adult.)

3. Take this picture of the logical, rational you and mentally shrink it down to a small dot in the bottom left hand corner of your mental screen.
4. See the first picture of the person about to start their difficult behaviour.
5. As you imagine the person starting to be difficult (e.g. they get 'that' look on their face) take the picture of the 'rational' you and expand it very fast so that it completely covers the first picture, so that all you can see and feel is you being calm as they run their 'difficult' behaviour pattern.
6. Shrink the picture of you in the Adult back down to a dot.
7. Bring back the image of the person about to start being difficult and then immediately zoom the Adult picture of you back to full size so it completely fills your mental screen.

Do this five or six times in rapid succession and finish on the picture of you 'in the adult', looking calm and objective, filling your mental screen.

If you do this exercise well you will find that as soon as you encounter a difficult person in 'real life' this image of the calm, logical you will zoom back to you and you will step into and stay in your Adult ego state with little or no conscious effort.

Interrupt their Pattern

Once we know (i) what the difficult persons 'game' is and (ii) have clarified what specifically it is we want to be different, the next step is to interrupt the difficult persons pattern of behaviour. There are three ways of doing this:

1. Stop it before it starts

If the person has a very clearly defined trigger or 'hot button' that kicks off their difficult behaviour it may be possible to avoid pressing the button. For example, say a manager shouts and bullies employees when they feel that they are not in control of a situation. It may be that just by keeping them informed of problems as soon as they occur they will never feel that he has to move into their Critical Parent pattern.

2. Mirror their pattern

Mirroring the persons pattern means that we 'get in step' with them by agreeing with them at a physical and emotional level. Since they will be expecting disagreement this is very confusing for them and it causes them to put their habitual pattern 'on hold'. To mirror the person we copy:

   a. The volume of their voice
   b. Their posture
   c. Their 'meta message' (i.e. we reflect the same emotion and feeling as they do but we do not agree with the content or meaning of their message.)

For example, suppose someone is being aggressive and shouting, yelling and brow beating you. They turn around and snarl the words '"Well that was a pretty stupid way to behave in a meeting!" You could, stay in your Adult and then:

Stand or sit like they are standing or sitting, talk at the same volume as they are and match the emotion of the underlying message, by saying something like:

> "Yes, I can see that you think that it was a pretty stupid way to behave."

Notice that while this agrees with their emotional state it does not 'give in to them' because we are not agreeing with the content. (You are not agreeing that you had behaved stupidly only that you can see that they believe that.) Thus, by agreeing with some part of what they say (the meta message) we confuse the other person and still retain our point of view and our integrity. This 'mirroring' of the persons pattern is often called the fogging technique.

3. Mismatch their pattern

In mismatching we seek to destroy the pattern the other person is trying to use by adopting a:

1. Voice tone
2. Body posture
3. 'Meta message'

Something which is utterly different from what is expected

So, for example imagine what would happen if someone was behaving aggressively towards you and you:

1. Yawned in a bored looking manner, or
2. Laughed out loud, or
3. Dropped on all fours and rolled over like a dog saying 'please don't beat me master', or
4. Got up and walked out the room, or
5. Said "do you know how much it upsets me when you talk to me like this", or
6. Blew them a kiss, or
7. Said, "Stop, Stop", or
8. Put your pen on your desk, stand up and take a step towards them, or
9. Say, "that reminds me of a story" and start to tell them an anecdote, or
10. Start to talk about how their behaviour makes you feel - the feelings commentary technique. E.g. "Do you realise how angry it makes me feel when you talk to me in that tone of voice?"

Of course which, if any, of these 'pattern interrupts' you try will depend on the person you are dealing with and your relationship with them. But they will all cause the other person to pause what they are doing while they try and come to terms with this unexpected response.

Use the 3 step Assertiveness Technique

Interrupting the person's pattern provides a brief window of opportunity, perhaps no more than one or two seconds, when you have a chance to take the lead. We take this lead by using the three step assertive pattern as outlined below but first we need to clarify what we mean by assertiveness.

What is Assertiveness?

Assertiveness is based on a philosophy of personal responsibility and an awareness of the rights of other people; being assertive means being honest with yourself and others. It means having the ability to say directly what it is you want, you need or you feel, but not at the expense of other people.

It means having confidence in yourself and being positive, while at the same time understanding other people's points of view. It means being able to behave in a rational and adult way. Being assertive means being able to negotiate and reach agreement(s) based on workable compromises. Above all, being assertive means having self-respect and respect for other people. It is based on starting in the Adult ego state and in adopting the beliefs of expert communicators outlined earlier in the manual.

To use the three steps you first interrupt the other person's pattern by mirroring or mismatching them. Then check that you are in your Adult ego state (which includes using a firm but even tone of voice and a relaxed, body posture.) Then:

1. Say something which shows we have heard and understood the other person's point of view.

2. Say what you think or feel.

3. Say what you would like to happen next.

In brief we say:

I understand that you would like ....
However, I feel ....
Therefore I suggest..........................

It takes all three steps to handle situations assertively, and to cope with difficult people rationally rather than emotionally.

Step three is essential so that you can indicate in a clear and straightforward way what action or outcome you want, without hesitancy or insistence. This is where time spent on clarifying your outcome earlier on in the process is invaluable.

Workable Compromise

In many situations that arise getting a resolution means that some compromises have to be struck, so that everyone gets at least some of what they want without damaging the interests of the other party: this is what we call 'workable compromise'. When we use the 'three steps' in handling a difficult person we must take care not to lose sight of the fact that some give and take may be necessary if we are to reach our desired outcome.

Maintain the relationship

Relationships need reinforcement to survive. This is achieved by 'staying in touch'. The issue here is getting the balance right, too much contact and the relationship can be 'swamped', too little and it dies. The amount of contact depends on needs, ours and theirs. With family, this for most of us means regular contact, with friends and business associates it's normally driven by common interests with others, particularly potential clients it depends on need, most importantly on their need.

Supporting relationships is like looking after plants. Plants need food, water and the climate relevant to their needs if they are to prosper, so do our relationships.

How we stay in touch is also important. It can be the card at Christmas, the occasional visit, 'I'm in the area and wondered if you'd like to come for lunch' the quarterly newsletter, a telephone call, Email etc. All you are doing saying 'Hello, I'm still here if you need me' and vice versa of course.

Developing your Relationship Management Skills

The self-development model used in this book is based on the following principles:

We already have role models within our minds which dictate how we behave when faced with different interpersonal situation. These provide us with a 'process' for handling a specific situation, a meeting, and interview, a presentation etc., a set of skills specific to the situation and our attitudes, based on our values, towards the situation. We all have our own ways of handling an interview for example, a meeting, a disciplinary situation etc. This is our natural behaviour, some of which is appropriate to optimising the specific situation and some of which is not. Note. It is important recognise that all of us have behaviours which make us naturally good at some human interactions but few of us are naturally masters of all interactive situations. It is these behaviours which are not natural to us that we need to learn.

Improvement starts with measurement. 'What we cannot, or do not measure, we cannot manage'. We have created benchmarking tools for the main areas of human interaction. We have done this by observing people who are naturally good at handling different interpersonal situations, recording what they do and how they do it, the skills they employ. These are our 'role models' the people who we need to emulate if we want to optimise our own performance. They are easy to see in sport , for example sport; if one wants to learn how to 'bend' a football we need to look no further then David Beckham as a role model. For improving our golf we have a perfect role model in Jack Nicholas and so on. To improve our driving skills we need look no further than Lewis Hamilton and so on. So to improve our interpersonal skills we need to find role models to emulate.

Improving means changing; some of the things we currently do will not be appropriate to what we wish to achieve in the future. To develop ourselves we must firstly be prepared to 'recognise' that we could become better interviewers, presenters, problem solvers etc. Secondly we must be willing to commit the time and effort necessary to achieve the desired change. Thirdly we must analyse the gap that separates us from optimum performance and be prepared to work to achieve our desired change.

Improving performance is an iterative process. Start with a benchmark. Measure your current performance against it. Identify the key things you need to improve and produce a plan to work on them. On completion of the plan again check your performance against the benchmark. If you have achieved your desired performance goals stop, if not go through the process again and continue until satisfied.

If we take golf as an example, the benchmark would be my handicap. Let's say that my handicap at the start of the process is 22 and I would like it to be 15. I go to see the course professional, in this case he or she is my 'role model' who, after watching me play, advises me that I need to improve my long game. This means plenty of practice on the driving range followed by regular games. For the next four weeks I practice on the range three times a week, 100 balls a time and Saturday and Sunday I play a round of golf. By the end of four weeks my handicap is holding steady at 18. I go back to the professional who advises me that I now need to improve my short game. . For the next four weeks I practice on the putting green three times a week, 100 balls a time and Saturday and Sunday I play a round of golf. By the end of four weeks my handicap is down to 15.

In our case the benchmark is an 'expert' model based on over thirty years' experience of working with and training people in relationship skills. Whilst our focus is on self-assessment we would strongly encourage you to seek other's views where this is practical in order to ensure that the feedback is objective. Once you have assessed yourself and analysed the results we provide you with planning proforma and some general guidance on how to create a performance improvement plan. At this stage we would also encourage you to look at the sections on Barriers to Building Effective Relationships and Relating to Everyone - The Beliefs Required. Implement your plan, review results, adjust the plan and continue until you are satisfied with achievements.

So let's get started.

Benchmarking

To create a 'benchmark' we need a framework for assessing how someone handles a difficult relationship. This framework is defined through pre meeting discussions, observation and reviews with 'experts' handling dialogues with people with whom there are difficult relationships. Our research shows that these people follow a seven-step approach:

1. Be aware what is going on – If you have a difficult relationship with someone it must be for a reason. The first step in resolving the difficulty therefore is to find out why it's difficult.

2. Understand the problem – What is the real issue that makes this relationship difficult? Is it me, I haven't communicated clearly, something I represent? Or, something inside them?
3. Know your outcome – Think through what you want from this relationship. What's in it for them? Try to find a workable compromise, something that will give both parties some of what they want.
4. Move to your Adult Ego state (see Further Reading for more information on Transactional Analysis) – Be calm, rational and objective, avoid being emotional or treating the other party like a child.
5. Interrupt their pattern – work to establish rapport by interrupting their behavioural pattern in a constructive way. I know you are unhappy about the way things are going, so let us look again at the situation and see if we can find a better way of working.
6. Use the 3 step Assertiveness Technique to manage the situation (see Annex B) Assertiveness will help you to create an adult relationship. One in which you can both focus on reaching a mutually satisfactory solution without the baggage of the past or the fears of the future.
7. Maintain the relationship – Agree how you will continue to support the relationship in the future. This could involve regular meetings or briefings, telephone calls etc.

We have used these categories to create a method for objectively assessing how you handle difficult relationships.

Categories	Points for assessment	Notes	Score
Awareness	Do you put the other person at ease? Are you able to read the 'meta' message? Do you explore behavioural issues? Do you successfully 'match'		

		behaviours to develop rapport?		
Understand the issues	Do you ask questions to identify the real issue? Do you test their understanding?			
Desired Outcomes	Do you have a clear plan for your desired outcomes? Is this aimed at a win / win solution? Was the plan acceptable to the other person?			
Adult behaviour	Do you operate from your 'adult' ego state? Body posture, upright, non-threatening? Do you maintain Even voice tone?			
Interrupt the pastern	Do you break the pattern? Work to achieve rapport? Control the discussion to keep it on track?			
Assertiveness	Do you use the 3 step approach Use broken record where appropriate? Offer workable compromise?			
Maintain Relationships	Do you agree the next steps? Agree follow up? Close the dialogue with 'thank you'?			
Assessment	Do you feel that you achieved your objective? How do you feel about your interpersonal skills Is everyone clear what happens next?			

Score:- Good – OK, Satisfactory - SAT, Needs Improvement - NI

Now is the time for you to assess yourself. Please consider the last difficult discussion you had and write comments against each question in the comment box. When you have responded to all questions in a box, review your comments and see whether you are Good, Satisfactory or Need Improvement and enter your score accordingly. If appropriate ask two or three people who you have some difficulty with to also complete and assessment form.

Analysing your assessment to identify development needs

Having completed your assessment the next step is to analyse it, what do the results mean and what can we do about them. To help you with this task we have create three simple case studies based on some of the more common needs identified when managing difficult relationships. Please read the following cases before you start your own assessment.

Case 1

Categories	Points for assessment	Notes	Score
Awareness	Did the interviewer demonstrate awareness of behavioural issues	Yes good awareness	OK
	Did they 'read' the nonverbal behaviour correctly?	Yes	
	Was behaviour 'matched' to develop rapport?	Yes – well done	
Understand the issues	Did the interviewer ask questions to identify the real issue?	Fair – needs more probing	NI
	Did they test their understanding?	No – needs to played back	
Desired Outcomes	Did the interviewer demonstrate a desire to reach a win / win solution?	Yes – worked hard to convince the other person of the value	Sat
	Was there evidence of a plan?	Yes	
Adult Behaviour	Body posture, upright, non-threatening	Fair – more nurturing parent than adult	NI
	Even voice tone?		
Interrupt the pattern	Did the interviewer change the direction of the conversation Control the discussion to keep it on track?	Yes – pushed it to his own agenda Yes – bit too strong. Needs more	NI

		involvement	
Assertiveness	Used the 3 step approach Used broken record where appropriate? Offered workable compromise	Yes – but in a NP way Yes – good ? not sure there was real buy in	NI
Maintain relationship	Did you agree the next steps? Agree follow up? Close the dialogue with 'thank you'?	Partially Yes Yes	Sat
Assessment	Did they achieve their objective? What impression are you now left with of their interpersonal skills? Are you clear what happens next?	Partially – got a result but not sure how committed the other party is Good but too much NP Yes	NI

This individual has good interpersonal skills, he / she is sensitive to the needs of others but at the same time is objective about his own needs. They made good use of the assertiveness techniques for selling their proposed solution that was accepted by the other party. His / her weakness is that being naturally strongly nurturing parent (NP) they use their good interpersonal skills to convince others of the 'rightness' of their proposed solution. This is fine when others accept it, but will, from time to time lead to both conflict and mistakes. This person needs to develop their ability to explore what others think and feel about things and to involve them in the decision making process. Participation leads to understanding, which creates commitment.

Case 2

Categories	Points for assessment	Notes	Score
Awareness	Did the interviewer demonstrate awareness of behavioural issues Did they 'read' the nonverbal behaviour correctly? Was behaviour 'matched' to develop rapport?	Yes – possibly too sensitive to them Yes – subconsciously! No – unfortunately she 'showed' him that he could bully her	NI
Understand the issues	Did the interviewer ask questions to identify the real issue?	No – Tried to but couldn't get through	NI

	Did they test their understanding?	No – as above	
Desired Outcomes	Did the interviewer demonstrate a desire to reach a win / win solution? Was there evidence of a plan?	Partially – Not knowing the real problem made it difficult Yes – some but not achieved	NI
Adult Behaviour	Body posture, upright, non-threatening Even voice tone?	No - More like adaptive child	NI
Interrupt the pattern	Did the interviewer change the direction of the conversation Control the discussion to keep it on track?	She tried but the other party was too aggressive Not really	NI
Assertiveness	Used the 3 step approach Used broken record where appropriate? Offered workable compromise	Partially – she tried but was not able to maintain it	NI
Maintain relationship	Did you agree the next steps? Agree follow up? Close the dialogue with 'thank you'?	No No No	NI
Assessment	Did they achieve their objective? What impression are you now left with of their interpersonal skills?	No – needs to learn to manage bullying Good sensitivity, poor control Needs to learn	NI

| | Are you clear what happens next? | to be assertive | |

Score:- Good – OK, Satisfactory - SAT, Needs Improvement – NI

This was an extremely difficult discussion. The other party has clearly created a successful career by bullying people weaker than themselves into giving them their own way. Mary had a good plan and tried to 'manage' the situation but was not strong enough. The first learning point from this experience is that when under attack as Mary was, the most appropriate action is to stop the dialogue. Take some time out. Go and think about what happened. Speak to someone who you feel can help. Re-plan, practice being assertive, get someone to role-play the other party for you, and then try again.

Remember, we are all our maker's children and each of us has the right to be. It is also worth knowing that bullies rarely show their true colours in front of the third party. So, if it's appropriate think about taking someone along to the next meeting

Case 3

Categories	Points for assessment	Notes	Score
Awareness	Did the interviewer demonstrate awareness of behavioural issues	Yes – good awareness	Sat
	Did they 'read' the nonverbal behaviour correctly?	Yes	
	Was behaviour 'matched' to develop rapport?	Yes – developed good rapport	
Understand the issues	Did the interviewer ask questions to identify the real issue?	Yes – used good open questions	Sat
	Did they test their understanding?	Yes	
Desired Outcomes	Did the interviewer demonstrate a desire to reach a win / win solution?	Yes	Sat
	Was there evidence of a plan?	Yes	
Adult Behaviour	Body posture, upright, non-threatening Even voice tone?	Yes – good use of adult behaviour	Sat
Interrupt the pattern	Did the interviewer change the direction of the conversation Control the discussion to keep it on track?	Yes Yes – nice light touch	Sat
Assertiveness	Used the 3 step approach Used broken record where appropriate? Offered workable	Yes – simple proposal, easy to understand and repeat Yes	Sat

	compromise		
Maintain relationship	Did you agree the next steps? Agree follow up? Close the dialogue with 'thank you'?	Yes – meeting next week Ongoing Yes	Sat
Assessment	Did they achieve their objective? What impression are you now left with of their interpersonal skills? Are you clear what happens next?	Yes – reached a mutually satisfactory agreement Good Yes	Sat

Score:- Good – OK, Satisfactory - SAT, Needs Improvement - NI

Michael has a natural ability to utilise adult behaviour. He is very comfortable with the process and used the assertiveness techniques very effectively. It has been a pleasure to work with him.

Now it's your turn. Look at what you have said about yourself and select the area(s) where you feel improvement would be most beneficial.
Use the following proforma to help you clarify your findings.

Strengths – the things I am good at	Weakness – things I need to improve

Barriers to Effective Interpersonal Relationships

Problems occur in interpersonal relationships when one party wants, or the other party believes they want, to change the status quo. The barriers, which are many, are the things that get in the way of negotiating a win / win change. These barriers are within us and within the other party. They are based on our 'beliefs' about ourselves and others. These beliefs are 'programmed' in during our formative years. Some are taught and others are learned. Taught beliefs are those things that the authority figures in our childhood decreed were good or bad. Some of the things we were taught are appropriate in later life; we should respect our elders but not to the degree where it stops us from constructively challenging mistakes or unfair behaviour. We should avoid eating things which are bad for us but not be so closed that we are afraid to try another nation's cuisine. It's all a matter of degree. As children we need guidance on what is right and wrong, but not to the degree where it creates barriers to openness. The following are just some of the 'taught' barriers created within us in childhood which are inappropriate to our later lives particularly in managing difficult relationships:-

I believe that it is important to:

1. avoid experiencing pain
2. never feel guilty, angry, or competitive
3. never to hurt anybody

4. be liked and accepted by everybody
5. do everything perfectly
6. be self-sufficient and do not rely on others
7. never to make a mistake
8. never challenge an authority figure
9. avoid conflict at all costs
10. attack (anger) is the best means of defence
11. if in doubt shout
12. pretend to agree, then do what you would like

Any one of these barriers can 'get in the way' of open and honest communication and hence severely limit a person's ability to handle a difficult relationships. For example, an individual who wants to avoid 'conflict' may find it very hard to face up to someone who uses Critical Parent based bullying tactics. Fortunately because all of us have the Adult ego state as part of our personality we have the capability to:

1. identify any unhelpful beliefs from our past
2. stop using them in the present
3. install new and more useful beliefs

One way of doing this is to:

1. Identify a past situation that you have had with a 'difficult relationship' and where you would like things to have been different.
2. Ask yourself: "What were my 'beliefs' that that got in the way of me getting the results that I would have liked to have?"
3. Consider how this belief could be modified or changed in the light of the 'expert' beliefs listed below.
4. Decide to start to use this new belief and to 'drop' the old one.
5. Mentally rehearse putting the new belief into practice. Use your imagination journey back to a time before the incident

that you have been thinking about happened. This time however take with you (i) your 'new' belief and, (ii) a feeling of confidence that you can do better than before. Use the new 'belief' to change what is happening in that incident. Notice the difference it makes when you act in accordance with this new belief. Run through the incident making changes to what is happening as many times as you need to in order to get a sense of having completely absorbed the belief into your way of thinking. This shows how different things can be from now on.
6. Quickly double check that the 'new' belief is a 'good' one for you.

Reward yourself every time you make a decision based on this new belief e.g. tell yourself 'well done' and give yourself a pat on the back.

Beliefs of 'expert' relationship managers

1. We all have the right to negotiate for what we want
2. Aim for workable compromise – win / win solutions give both parties at least some of what they want
3. Value what we have – we have a good relationship don't let us destroy it over one issue
4. Know your outcome – be clear what you want
5. Know your BATNA (Best Alternative to a Negotiated Agreement)
6. Work in the adult, don't allow emotions to cloud the issue
7. Test understanding
8. Take a break if you are becoming deadlocked
9. Value differences and encourage others to do the same
10. Be realistic – tell it the way it is and be content with what is possible
11. Be prepared to apologise if you get it wrong.

Create a development plan

Having decided what you want to work on the next step is to create a plan. The plan allows you to visualise what you need to do to achieve your desired improvements and provides a useful vehicle for both control and sharing this information with others. Your plan needs to set out what you will do, by when and how you will assess your achievement.

The following example is taken from case 2

PERSONAL ACTION PLAN

Name ...Mary Robinson........ Start Date 3rd September..... End Date....End October......

Title of Project: - Using Adult Behaviour
Purpose: What do you want to achieve through the action? To develop my ability to use adult behaviour when trying to reach an agreement in a difficult relationship. I would like to feel comfortable in my adult and to use this to stop myself being bullied by people with strong personalities.
Current Situation: Where are you now? I did plan what I wanted to achieve but was unable use it. Bill was aggressive from the start and I was unable to get through. I was so stressed by the situation that I forgot what I planned to say. I need to develop a simple message and use the assertiveness techniques to deliver it until I am listened to. I

need to develop my self-confidence and believe that the only way is through practice. I will try to get some training in Assertiveness and see if my friend George in HR will help me practice.

Actions: What actions do you plan to undertake? By when? (Please be specific about dates)
Ask George about assertiveness training and help – Today
Go on training – soon – within two weeks
Agree practice with George - 1st week back after the training
Review results and decide next steps – Have arranged further meeting with Bill for end September
Note. Our experience shows that for most people, a training course followed by a concentrated period of supported practice like the one outlined in this plan will be sufficient to give the learner the self-confidence they need to apply the learning.

Resources: What resources do you have to help you achieve your outcome? How can you make best use of them?
Assertiveness training
Help from Anna
A Video which I can use to record my practice session for analysis
The benchmarking form from this manual.

Desired Outcome: What are you aiming to achieve? How do you want things to be different? What specifically will you see, hear and feel when you have finished that you don't see, hear and feel now?

I will be better able to manage difficult relationships successfully if I plan my outcomes and negotiate in my adult using the assertiveness technique.

Results: How have things turned out? What have you learnt from the experience of working on the project?

Now it's your turn. Complete the following Personal Action Plan for yourself.

PERSONAL ACTION PLAN

Name .... Start Date .... End Date...........................

Title of Project:
Purpose: What do you want to achieve through the action?
Current Situation: Where are you now?
Actions: What actions do you plan to undertake? By when? (Please be specific about dates)
Resources: What resources do you have to help you achieve your outcome? How can you make best use of them?
Desired Outcome: What are you aiming to achieve? How do you want things to be different? What specifically will you see, hear and feel when you have finished that you don't see, hear and feel now?
Results: How have things turned out? What have you learnt from the experience of working on the project?

Tips when creating your Plan

1. Start by listing the activities. The things you will do to achieve your development goals.
2. Identify key events. For this plan the most logical key events will be your actual presentations.
3. Create realistic time scales
4. Review to ensure it is do-able - Be realistic. Don't set your goals too high or they become de-motivating, too low or they have no value.
5. Don't try to do too much - Go for little and often. Remember the old saying 'How do you eat and Elephant? One bite at a time!
6. Use objective measures – things that can be objectively assessed. Things like, time, quantity, dates, results etc.
7. Create milestones, key events which you can use to track your progress.
8. Share it with someone. Sharing a plan makes it more powerful. You are more likely to see it through if you have someone who is going to ask you how it's going!
9. Use your plan to monitor your achievements.
10. Don't be afraid to update it if things change. It's a live document and should reflect where you are and where you are going.

Implementing your Plan

There are a number of factors which influence the success or failure of a Self-Development Plan:-

The main requirement is discipline; being committed to doing the work. Self-development plans are like diets, easy things to draw up but very difficult to stick to. This is basically because what we are now reflects our values, things we seek and the things we seek to avoid. I weight 100 kilos because I like good food, enjoy a social drink and would rather watch TV or read a book in the evenings that go to the gym. If I really wanted to be 75 kilos I would have to change my life style, deny myself those things I like and start doing things that I don't like.

One of the most powerful motivators for people is fear of looking a fool, which incidentally is why so many people don't like making presentations! And, whilst this is of itself a negative emotion it can be and is used positively to help people who want to change. It is the core driver for self-help groups like Weight Watchers, Alcoholics Anonymous, Stop Smoking and thousands more. Such groups have good results because the majority of members don't want to let each other down. You can also use this emotion to help you win through. If you can find else who wants to develop their presentation skills and agree to work together coaching and supporting each other. This is very effective because neither party wants to appear foolish in the eyes of the other. The next best thing is to find a coach. Someone you respect who has some experience of presenting and ask them to help you by giving feedback and support. This is also effective because you are no longer alone.

Don't be too rigid about the plan

Be prepared to make changes as you go along. The main thing is to stay focused on your desired outcome. If you want to be a competent presenter, then do what is necessary to make this happen.

a round of golf. By the end of four weeks my handicap is down to 15.

In our case the benchmark is an 'expert' model based on over thirty years' experience of working with and training people in relationship skills. Whilst our focus is on self-assessment we would strongly encourage you to seek other's views where this is practical in order to ensure that the feedback is objective. Once you have assessed yourself and analysed the results we provide you with planning proforma and some general guidance on how to create a performance improvement plan. At this stage we would also encourage you to look at the sections on Barriers to Building Effective Relationships and Relating to Everyone - The Beliefs Required. Implement your plan, review results, adjust the plan and continue until you are satisfied with achievements.

So let's get started.

Now it's your turn. Complete the following Personal Action Plan for yourself.

PERSONAL ACTION PLAN

Name .... Start Date .... End Date..............................

Title of Project:
Purpose: What do you want to achieve through the action?
Current Situation: Where are you now?
Actions: What actions do you plan to undertake? By when? (Please be specific about dates)
Resources: What resources do you have to help you achieve your outcome? How can you make best use of them?
Desired Outcome: What are you aiming to achieve? How do you want things to be different? What specifically will you see, hear and feel when you have finished that you don't see, hear and feel now?
Results: How have things turned out? What have you learnt from the experience of working on the project?

Tips when creating your Plan

11. Start by listing the activities. The things you will do to achieve your development goals.
12. Identify key events. For this plan the most logical key events will be your actual presentations.
13. Create realistic time scales
14. Review to ensure it is do-able - Be realistic. Don't set your goals too high or they become de-motivating, too low or they have no value.
15. Don't try to do too much - Go for little and often. Remember the old saying 'How do you eat and Elephant? One bite at a time!
16. Use objective measures – things that can be objectively assessed. Things like, time, quantity, dates, results etc.
17. Create milestones, key events which you can use to track your progress.
18. Share it with someone. Sharing a plan makes it more powerful. You are more likely to see it through if you have someone who is going to ask you how it's going!
19. Use your plan to monitor your achievements.
20. Don't be afraid to update it if things change. It's a live document and should reflect where you are and where you are going.

Implementing your Plan

There are a number of factors which influence the success or failure of a Self-Development Plan:-

The main requirement is discipline; being committed to doing the work. Self-development plans are like diets, easy things to draw up but very difficult to stick to. This is basically because what we are now reflects our values, things we seek and the things we seek to avoid. I weight 100 kilos because I like good food, enjoy a social drink and would rather watch TV or read a book in the evenings that go to the gym. If I really wanted to be 75 kilos I would have to change my life style, deny myself those things I like and start doing things that I don't like.

One of the most powerful motivators for people is fear of looking a fool, which incidentally is why so many people don't like making presentations! And, whilst this is of itself a negative emotion it can be and is used positively to help people who want to change. It is the core driver for self-help groups like Weight Watchers, Alcoholics Anonymous, Stop Smoking and thousands more. Such groups have good results because the majority of members don't want to let each other down. You can also use this emotion to help you win through. If you can find else who wants to develop their presentation skills and agree to work together coaching and supporting each other. This is very effective because neither party wants to appear foolish in the eyes of the other. The next best thing is to find a coach. Someone you respect who has some experience of presenting and ask them to help you by giving feedback and support. This is also effective because you are no longer alone.

Don't be too rigid about the plan

Be prepared to make changes as you go along. The main thing is to stay focused on your desired outcome. If you want to be a competent presenter, then do what is necessary to make this happen.

Continuous assessment

We said earlier that what we can't or don't measure we cannot manage. To help you manage your progress during the implementation phase of your Inter-Personal Relationship Development Plan we have included methodology for assessing your progress, see below. You should complete this form after each intervention.   Continually assess where you are in relation to the goals you have set yourself. Be prepared to adjust your goals in line with the realities of the situation. Recognise that it's not possible as the saying goes 'to win them all'. If you're not succeeding with one approach, try something else. Stay focused, stay motivated and be realistic.

RELATIONSHIP DEVELOPMENT PLAN
SELF-ASSESSMENT

Be aware of what is going on Describe in detail what you see and hear the person do when they are difficult. Can you spot the 'trigger' for their difficult behaviour?	
Understand the problem Why do you think the person acts as they do?	

Know your Outcome Understand how, when and where you want things to be different. Think about how this goal fits in with your other goals. Set specific dates and times for taking action.	
Move to your Adult ego state Rehearse being calm, relaxed and objective when you deal with the difficult person. Think about how you need to change in order to deal more effectively with the other person.	
Interrupt their pattern Think of at least three ways in which you can interrupt the person's behaviour pattern.	
Use the 3 step Assertiveness Technique Write out a script for each of the three steps to use with the difficult person. Rehearse using it both mentally and with a colleague.	

Annex A - Profiles of Difficult People

On the following pages are outline profiles of some of the more common patterns of 'difficult people' and some ideas for dealing with them. It is not exhaustive and it is important to be flexible in your approach in 'real life' situations. There are for example many more 'reasons' for people being difficult than those listed here and many more ways of successfully interrupting patterns. The profiles do, however, give some guidance on how to tackle the difficult people that are most commonly found in organisations.

Aggressive

Process Step	Comments & Example Actions
Be aware of what is going on	Loud voice, harsh condescending tone, hectoring bullying behaviour. No interest in listening or talking about things. Says things like "This is rubbish!" and "What the Hell did you think you were doing?"
Understand the problem	They are driven by a Parent need to be right. They want to push you into an Adaptive child ego state so that you feel submissive and unable to stand up to them.
Know your Outcome	To get them to listen to your point of view.
Move to your Adult ego state	Get a sense of being calm, relaxed and objective.
Interrupt their pattern	Stand up Say "I'm not sure that you heard what I was really trying to say"
Use the 3 step Assertiveness Technique	I understand that you have strong views on this However I feel that we need to talk it through in more detail I suggest we go over the main points again

Testers

Process Step	Comments & Example Actions
Be aware of what is going on	They make sarcastic or snide comments about you, sometimes under the cover of a 'joke', often to other people but just loud enough for you to hear.
Understand the problem	A critical Parent response motivated by a strong sense of what you should be doing. Relies on your Adaptive Child conditioning in social 'rules' and conventions to prevent you from addressing the attack directly.
Know your Outcome	To develop a more open relationship.
Move to your Adult ego state	Be relaxed and objective. Focus on building a relationship
Interrupt their pattern	Use open questions, explore issues but don't get into debate; focus on why?"
Use the 3 step Assertiveness Technique	I understand that you see this as a problem However I am not sure you are right I suggest we try to clarify exactly what you feel about xxx' Use 'Broken Record' as necessary

Exploders

Process Step	Comments & Example Actions
Be aware of what is going on	Sudden, violent loss of self-control. Loud, shrill voice.
Understand the problem	This is a Free Child pattern based on the rebellious part of that ego state. The person quite literally loses control for a few minutes and flies into a rage.
Know your Outcome	Help them to calm down .
Move to your Adult ego state	Get a sense of being calm, relaxed and objective.
Interrupt their pattern	Say "Stop, Stop" Stand and say their name.
Use the 3 step Assertiveness Technique	I understand that this is important to you However I don't want to talk about it like this I suggest we have a five minute break and then start again

Talkers & Blamers

Process Step	Comments & Example Actions
Be aware of what is going on	They complain about you and other people but never take any constructive action. They often say things like "If you really (care about your people) you would...
Understand the problem	These people are Adaptive child. They have a strong sense of what is 'right' but also feel that they are powerless to change anything. They want you to feel responsible for the way they feel and do something about it.
Know your Outcome	To uncover the underlying problem and agree some action to address it.
Move to your Adult ego state	Be calm, relaxed, objective and persistent.
Interrupt their pattern	Say something like "OK, so what are we going to do about it?"
Use the 3 step Assertiveness Technique	I understand that you have strong views on this However I feel we need to get to the bottom of things Therefore I suggest we agree what action we can take to move things forward

Shy People

Process Step	Comments & Example Actions
Be aware of what is going on	These people are silent and unresponsive, avoiding eye contact and mumbling a few words in answer to questions.
Understand the problem	The shy person is working from their Adaptive Child ego state and is trying to 'be left alone'..
Know your Outcome	To get the person to start talking.
Move to your Adult ego state	Be objective, patient and interested.
Interrupt their pattern	Say "I want to help you but I can't do that if you don't say anything to me." Be patient and stay silent rather than feeling that you have to start to talk to 'fill the gap'
Use the 3 step Assertiveness Technique	I understand that you find it hard to discuss this However I feel that we need to talk it through in more detail So I want to know what I can do to help you to be more open with me. If they still don't respond try the 'broken record' technique. If all else fails schedule another meeting and try again.

Nice People

Process Step	Comments & Example Actions
Be aware of what is going on	Nice people always say, "yes" to you but then often don't get around to taking any action.
Understand the problem	These people use an Adaptive child based pattern where they feel a strong need for approval and dread the thought of upsetting people by saying "no" to them, in case they stop liking them.
Know your Outcome	Help the person to be honest and realistic.
Move to your Adult ego state	Be patient and encouraging but persistent.
Interrupt their pattern	Ask "How do you know that you'll get the job done on time?"
Use the 3 step Assertiveness Technique	I understand that you would like to help me with this and I want you to know that I really appreciate that However I need to be sure that you can deliver on time Therefore I suggest we review your priorities and make sure that you can fit this job in

Defenders

Process Step	Comments & Example Actions
Be aware of what is going on	Everything is a problem. I'm OK you're not Ok. It's not my fault.
Understand the problem	This is a pattern based on the Critical Parent ego state, which sees others actions as self-serving and poorly thought out. The aim is for the person to keep a sense of superiority because they 'know' and everyone else is wrong.
Know your Outcome	To encourage the person to assess the issues and if there is some truth in them and there often is, to take appropriate action
Move to your Adult ego state	Be calm, relaxed and objective.
Interrupt their pattern	When they make a proposal say "That's a good point, what do you think we should do about it?"
Use the 3 step Assertiveness Technique	I understand that you have reservations about the plan However I feel that they can be dealt with So I would like to hear your ideas on how we can move forward

Time wasters

Process Step	Comments & Example Actions
Be aware of what is going on	They offer support and seem positive about issues but fail to commit to action.
Understand the problem	These people may appear similar to 'Nice' people in their behaviour but the source of the pattern is different. Time wasting is a Nurturing Parent pattern where the person feels unable to move forward as a result they wait until the decision is made for them.
Know your Outcome	Help them to make decisions.
Move to your Adult ego state	Be calm, relaxed and objective.be prepared to challenge seek action
Interrupt their pattern	Say "Can you picture yourself implementing this decision and if you can how do you feel about it?"
Use the 3 step Assertiveness Technique	I understand that you feel that we need to proceed with care However I feel that we need to work to resolve this issue I suggest we talk about what factors are important in reaching a decision on the way forward

Avoiders

Process Step	Comments & Example Actions
Be aware of what is going on	Avoiders resist doing any more than the minimum. They say things like "I'm not being paid to do that".
Understand the problem	This is a Free Child pattern in which the person feels that any new task is an imposition to be resisted by a litany of excuses. Their goal to avoid taking on other duties.
Know your Outcome	To persuade them to accept responsibility for the whole job.
Move to your Adult ego state	Be calm, relaxed, objective and persistent..
Interrupt their pattern	Say "What other people do or don't do is not relevant. What is important is that the job needs doing and I want you to do it so lets talk about getting it done".
Use the 3 step Assertiveness Technique	I understand that you don't feel that this is your responsibility However I believe it is Therefore I suggest we agree when you will do it and what training, if any, you need. If they continue use the 'broken record technique'.

Further Reading

If you have found reading this book interesting you may also find the following useful.

1. For an insight into human behaviour I recommend Dr. Thomas A. Harris is the author of *I'm OK – You're OK*, the 1969 bestseller based upon the ideas of Transactional Analysis by **Dr Eric Berne**. ISBN 0-06-072427. If you find this interesting you may also like to read 'The Games People Play, by Dr Eric Berne ISBN 0-345-41003-3

2. In the same géndre but more focused on 'rapport' skills is NPL, How to Build a Successful Life by Richard Brandler, Alessio Roberti & Owen Fitzpatrick, published by Harper Collins, ISBN 978-0-00-749741-6

3. For a deeper understanding of values I suggest 'What Matters Most' by Hyrum W Smith, published by Franklin Covey Co. ISBN 0-684-87256-0

4. For an entertaining insight into the real world of influencing I recommend the book 'When I Stop Talking You'll Know I'm Dead by Jerry Weintraub, Rich Cohen and George Clooney, Published by Hachette Books ISBN 978-0-446-54815-1

5. To learn more about 'action learning' I recommend Reg's original book on the subject 'The ABC of Action Learning' Published by Gower Publications, ISBN 978-1-4094-2703-2 Mike Pedlars Action Learning in Practice, Third Edition, Ed Mike Pedler, Gower Press, ISBN 0 566 07795 7 and More than Management Development, Edited by David Casey & David Pearce, Gower Press, 1977. ISBN 0-566-022005-X This book reviews the early GEC programmes referred to in this text.

6. If you would like to learn more about Facilitation then 'Facilitating Action Learning: A Practitioner's Guide' by **Mike Pedler** and **Christine Abbott** is a useful read. Also David Casey's excellent paper on The Emerging Role of the Set Advisers, copies available from ALA International

Books George has written on Action Learning and related topics

The following books are published by ALA International. They are available on our web site www.ala-international.com and from **Google Books** and **Amazon** in Epub or paperback formats.

Books about Action learning

Applications of Action Learning – describes the philosophy of action learning and its applications. ISBN 978-0-9560822-4-4

In-Plant Action Learning – explains how the philosophy of Action learning can be used to deliver organisational change. ISBN 978-0-9560822-3-7

In-Plant Action Learning Teams, Participants Guide – This Guide is designed to help In-Plant teams to self-manage and facilitate their own learning; available from ALA International.

Empowering Change Through Facilitation – describes facilitation as applied in Action Learning programmes. ISBN 978-0 -9560822-9-9

Books about Personal Development

Managers as Leaders - This book show how management and leadership combine to ensure the effective delivery of the task. ISBN 978-0-9560822-2-0

Managing Difficult Relationships – examines the reasons for difficult relationships and provides a 'framework' for negotiating win / win solutions. ISBN 978-0-9560822-5-1

Change; Become a Winner - I believe that life is not a rehearsal, it's a journey and you can change it. If you would like to do something different with your life this book is for you. ISBN 13 978-1503185401, ISBN 10:1503185400

Books about Productivity

Values & Style; the Key to Productivity –The common denominator in performance improvement in organizations, is managing style. The things that stop people doing the best job they can stem from 'them and us' attitudes. These are based on cultural values and determine the way human beings perceive their roles and relationships within hierarchies. This book explores the nature of values and style and how they impact the operating effectiveness of organizations and societies.

Re-Engineering the Workplace – This book describes the Japanese approach to productivity with practical examples on how it can be applied in practice.

Please use the following link to find these books on Amazon.

http://www.amazon.com/s?ie=UTF8&page=1&rh=n%3A2831 55%2Cp_27%3AGeorge%20Boulden

We will be very grateful if you will take a few minutes to review your thoughts on this book while you are there. Thank you.

George Boulden

www.ingramcontent.com/pod-product-compliance
Lightning Source LLC
Chambersburg PA
CBHW030954240526
45463CB00016B/2560